Dedication

to my childhood friend....

Through the noise of the crowd, I heard the quiet of you.

CONTENTS

Introduction. 8
Possibility. 10
Selfless Self. 12
Loneliness. 14
When To Love. 16
Those Who Have Left You. 18
Bitter Winter. 20
What Isn't There. 22
Contradictory Loss. 24
Being Left Behind. 26
Noticing. 28
Thinking. 30
Done and Never Done. 32
Melancholy. 34
Cure (for my parents). 36
A Beloved Face. 38
Powerful Tears. 40
Opening The Heart. 42
I'll Make It Through. 44
Alive. 46
Gentle. 48
You Are Beautiful. 50
The Precious Things You Do. 52
A Look Of Love. 54
Because Of You. 56
Something Beginning With You. 58
The One Who Wants To Stay. 60
You Are One Of My Reasons. 62
A Beautiful Day. 64
Mending. 66
How The World Works. 68
Cementing Our Views. 70
A Movement Has Begun. 72
Police Attack. 74
The Dying Living. 76
Bravery That Only Grows. 78

Righteousness. 80
Brainwashing. 82
Angry Concepts. 84
Ignorance. 86
We've Left Them. 88
Is It Humane? 90
The Children We Forgot. 92
Regrets. 94
Tear Trails. 96
Blood. 98
The Ways Of Our World. 100
Family. 102
Bare Minimum. 104
Little Dreamer. 106
Falling. 108
Quietness. 110
Genuine. 112
Wrongs and Rights. 114
The Intuitive Heart. 116
Trends. 118
Popularity. 120
What Isn't Love? 122
Quiet Presence, Present Mind. 124
Validation. 126
Do You Feel Complete? 128
Fear. 130
Finding. 132
Liberation. 134
The Education System. 136
The Day. 138
Powerful And Beautiful. 140
Difficulties. 142
Forgiving The Situation. 144
Hatred. 146
People Want To Hear Negativity. 148
Our Precious Languages. 150

To Listen Properly. 152
Learning Your Language. 154
Colours. 156
A Common Dismissal. 158
Culture. 160
Misconception. 162
All It Took. 164
A Captive Life. 166
Mixed Race. 168
Judgement. 170
Let's Move Forth Together. 172
Heartbeat. 174
To Truly Live. 176
Ballet Steps. 178
Soulmate Dance. 180
Where I Fall Weak for You. 182
Written. 184
Make Peace. 186
Courage. 188
The Truth About Trials. 190
The Path We are Afraid To Take. 192
The Heart And Mind. 194
Time. 196
Gratitude. 198
The Beauty Of Prayer. 200
The Trauma Identity. 202
Remember With Happiness. 204
Sign Language. 206
Inspiration And Solace. 208
Just Like The Sun. 210
Time To Grow. 212
A Bird In Flight. 214
Possible. 216
Now. 218

Acknowledgements. 220
About The Author. 222

Little Dreamer

By Ella Zelensky

© Ella Zelensky, 2021. All rights reserved

Introduction

The words you are about to read encompass universal experiences.
When we feel like we're falling apart, we tend to feel as though it's a personal problem and that we cannot be understood by others.
The truth is: heartbreak is felt by billions of others across the world.

But just like heartbreak, happiness can also be felt by billions of others too.
No matter what background we have or what time zone we're in, our brothers and sisters in humanity - across this beautiful planet - are sharing the same feelings as you.

What's precious about this is that we're all feeling these emotions at the same time without realising someone else is. Although our languages use different words for them, the emotion is still the same.

Nowadays, the world has come together so much more, offering further opportunities to learn about each other. Isn't it beautiful to think of all the shared experiences we've had since birth?

Once we remember and acknowledge that the emotions and adversities we have are shared universally, the idea of being able to survive them becomes so much more positive.

This book will speak of heartbreak, but it will also conclude with hope and new perspectives.

We are not alone - we are a whole world. We are each other.

May these words bring healing, and bring people together.

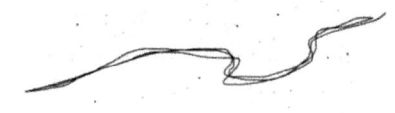

Possibility

There is no conclusion as we feel it to be,
but rather,
the subliminal arrival of possibility.

Selfless Self

I would rather
give my heart
than to see
another fall
for it's
the presence of
my selfless self
that bears a life
at all.

Loneliness

There are two kinds of loneliness…

1 – when you do the wrong thing, out of insecurity,
to those who do the right thing,
but you are met with good treatment anyway.

And 2 – when you do the right thing, out of no insecurity,
to those who do the wrong thing,
but you are met with horrible treatment anyway.

The first person attracts a group.

The second person attracts the world.

When To Love

You don't know when not to love,
but that is far greater than
never knowing how to.
It's love that people need, even if
you don't think they do.

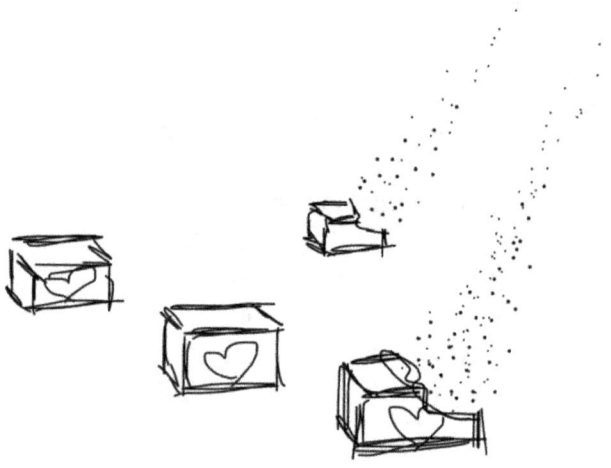

Those Who Have Left You

You gave parts of your soul away out of love. To give
the gift of love reflects your compassion. With the leaving of any
kind of relationship does not come the leaving of all of who you are.
What you give stays present in who you are. What they took
dwindles in their pride. Your tears come from your humanity,
and that is something you should be very proud of. There is
no other way but love, so in the face of every pain from hereon,
respond continually with that love.

Bitter Winter

Keep me safe
and never let me go
but if you must
regardless, I'll grow
love can be beautiful
surrounded in snow
as bitter winters harvest
the resilience we sow.

What Isn't There

Little love
in little care
don't entertain
what isn't there.

Contradictory Loss

How strange…
to grieve over someone I
haven't physically lost…
but emotionally have.

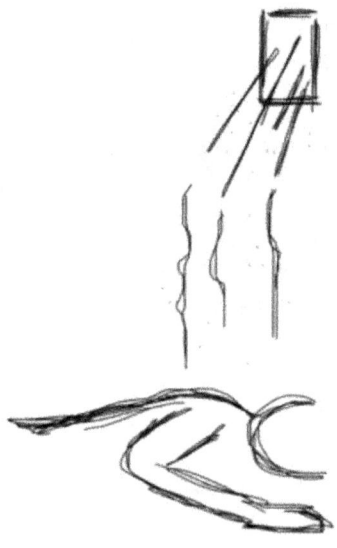

Being Left Behind

Precarious chair
my feet almost touch
the floor, bare
and scarcely invigorating
is the silver sunlight there
for I am caught in many places
within one place
without sensation or face
swaying to prompt for tears
to subside which
will not subside
in this strange and unknown where,
with a precarious chair,
my soul unwinds by
pull of lace in this
still and poignant space.

Noticing

Perhaps it is that I notice much and not speak
whilst others speak much and do not notice.

Thinking

Know that by day
I seem present and persistent
but know that by night
by the glow of candlelight
you will see the saddest me
ticking machinery
butterfly debris
enigmatic mystery
for I am lonely
and always will be.

Done And Never Done

The origin of pain
was never so close
to what was done
but to what was never done
in all that could have
unfurled beautifully
and could have stayed.

Melancholy

My mind often mistakes
melancholy for medicine.

Running through what has gone wrong in our lives does not inspire us to
make changes towards a happier future. Melancholy is not our medicine.
We are worth far more than standing next to what happened to us and
refusing to take steps away – steps of hope, and ultimately change.
Working towards feeling better shouldn't be something we fear
or think we're incapable of.

Cure (For My Parents)

There is only one cure
for the unkindness of living
it resides in your chest
the love you are giving.

A Beloved Face

How do I face
a beloved face
when I broke
the heart I adore
it wasn't my intention
these words
aren't inventions
I never meant
to hurt you more.

Powerful Tears

My tears are of such a quantity
that I would perhaps replenish the withering meadow.
Note: cry tears of courage.
To grow and rise above, never give up.

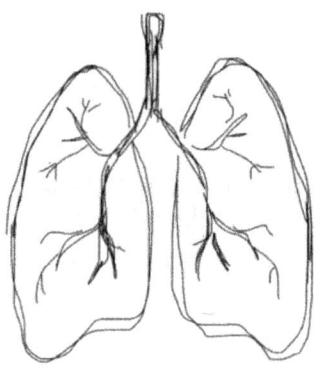

Opening The Heart

Prolonged disappearances sound soothing
until the fundamental need for company stands its ground
I wanted to hear words that reminded me of life,
but also not a sound
oxygen is beautiful, it reminds the heart to pound... so breathe.
If you open up your heart, you will someday be found.

I'll Make It Through

In the arms of sorrow
I fight for resurrection
but I'm locked in ice
in unbreakable protection
of inner sunlight
I feel detection
but it's trembling, now
it's dying, how
don't touch my hands
I need your vow
let go of me
the impending sounds
of oceanic creatures
swimming rounds
my cheeks hold a smile
you won't see for a while
come hold me
I want your touch
don't touch my soul
I bear too much
come fix my heart
my threshold is dying
stay away, I'm sorry, I'm trying
it's lonely here in the glimmering blue
but I'll make it through

if I see you.

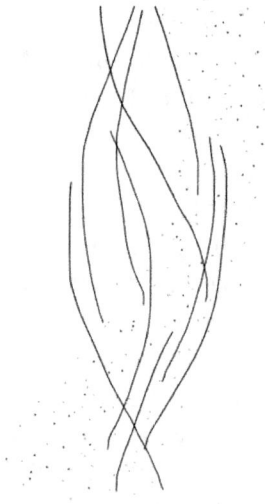

Alive

And sometimes
it is in
our most lifeless
moments
that we,
unknowingly,
are the most
alive.

Gentle

Don't fret for being gentle
such a beautiful gentle
heart you have
never believe otherwise
for it is a
gentle heart
that is wary
and a gentle heart
that is kind
a gentle heart is one

people truly listen to.

You Are Beautiful

If I stare at you gently and dearly
believe me, you are beautiful
if I watch you in happiness
believe me, you are beautiful
and if I approach you
when my heart frowns
believe me, you are beautiful
a beautiful friend and soul
someone attentive, compassionate
someone I hope one day
lifts up their eyes
to meet mine when I say
believe me…

The Precious Things You Do

I see you walking slowly over there
with gentleness in your footsteps
what is it that has you
walk so slowly?
And what is it about you
that makes my heart beat
so quickly?
It's the beauty you see in
the things you find
and you are so selfless,
so inexplicably kind
so how could someone
ever leave you behind?
So much wisdom, the way you talk
is beautiful, enrapturing, sincere
you easily have me cry a tear.

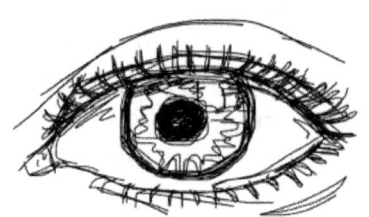

A Look Of Love

The love I wish to describe to you
is so profound that only my eyes
can convey it to you in a single moment.
That is why eyes are beautiful.

Because Of You

Beauty in your eyes
gentleness, there flows
and I'm forced to let go
each form of my pain dies
you say, I'm taking you
beyond the roads and towers
running past cities
to arrive at flowers
they say it isn't difficult
to notice sincere eyes
and remarkable it is
if in this world,
they remain alive
you say, forget belonging
it's an unnecessary longing
you say, live true
gorgeously, you are unaware
I began practicing this

because of you.

Something Beginning With You

I spy with
my captivated eyes
something beginning
with you
and all that you do
drips with grace
you stop the place
little words, though
you've said it all
and you're the kind
to fall when
another does
to those in need,
you are not blind.

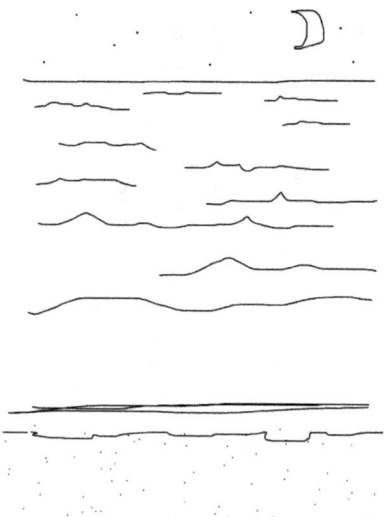

The One Who Wants To Stay

But so certain
they draw the curtain
in silence hid away
little do they know
of the one who wants to stay.

You Are One Of My Reasons

Live for moments where a friend
comes knocking on your door
with weighted eyes and scarce glow
and sit them down to let them know
that you love them
where there is love, there is reason
and you are one of my reasons.

A Beautiful Day

You say you are breaking
and I don't deny it
but even as you cry
I can see your tears
fuelling your passion
your determination
your love
I know you might
not see it now
but everything you do
is making you stronger
even your fragile moments
they're all adding up
to a beautiful day
which I assure you isn't
too far away
in fact, you could

make it today.

Mending

Though as your
paper soul flakes away
in beautiful decay
I shall walk your way
with strings attached
to my fingers
and attach them back to
all of you that soars away
from your make –
I shall thread each part
through its other,
then tug the final string
and smile to your eyes
with unwavering focus
as you mend.

How The World Works

And if that is how the world works,
then I would wish to take
no part in it, for I am not for
these behaviours and their consequences.
But I see hope in that this isn't always
how the world works… and if that is
so, then I would wish to take part in it, for
I value what is right in
the goodness of its opportunities.

Cementing Our Views

Some people are alarmingly passionate
about ploughing the field dead
for reason
upon reason
upon reason
to attack people they hate.

A Movement Has Begun

Wake up, there are fires burning
and people are yearning for peace
for no blood to be spilled
for the hate to cease
for no more lives to be killed
we're screaming their names
holding picture frames
but there are guns firing
and fists finding faces
so tie up your laces
it's time to run
a movement has begun
and will not fall until won.

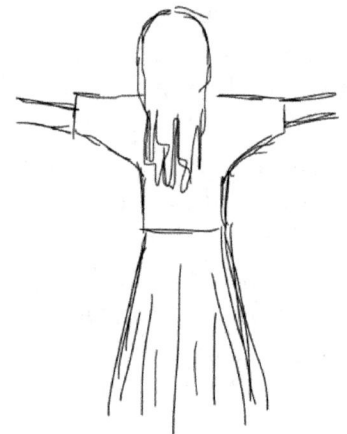

Police Attack

The crowd throws up their arms
and surges through the streets
like the fluidity of water
and of a fallen mother
you are the last daughter
your face turns back
before the police attack
and you look me so elegantly
so sure in the eyes
before the front row dies
and you were in the front row.

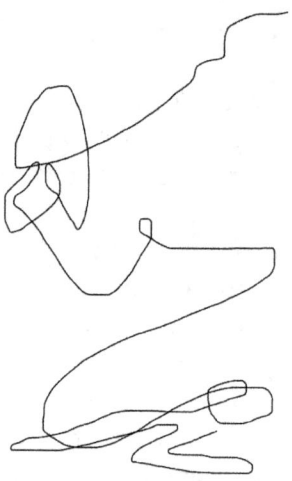

The Dying Living

Living souls are dying
for living over crying
at the dying living.

Bravery That Only Grows

You treat them as inferior
but little do you know
of their unbreakable faith
you don't fracture them
like you so desperately want to believe
they still wake up each morning
with bravery that only grows
with each passing day
and when their community unites
and cries in the streets for their people
you will never have the power
to contain that echo
because those who care echo it back
all around the world
it will live forever
like the love in their hearts
that remains even when you
make it your mission to cut them down
now that's a statement
that's an example
that's a community that knows
what humanity should be.

Righteousness

We raise our hands when asked if we value change
but step back when change actually calls for us
is righteousness really that embarrassing?

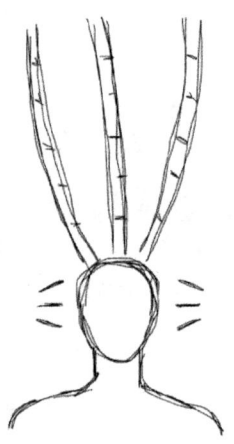

Brainwashing

Imagine reaching the end of our life and
maintaining a hatred for people
we haven't even truly met
brainwashing reprograms us into fearing
the very world we share. Unfortunately,
it controls multitudes of people's lifespans and
diverts them from one of the most beautiful
gifts of life: interracial, intercultural and
interfaith connection. There should be
no glass wall between our hands.

"They are dangerous because it gives me a thrill to see them as such."

Angry Concepts

People speak truths that
others are too proud to believe.
They're inconvenient to the angry concept
they love to think about.
Like many films, it enthrals,
and like many films, it is exaggerated,
and like many films, it isn't real.

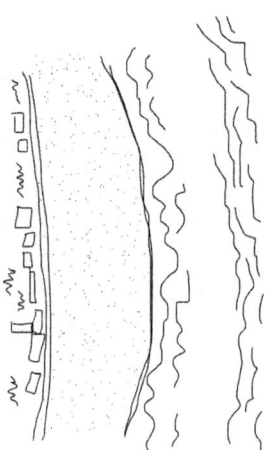

Ignorance

Many people in privileged countries
keep their mentalities behind their coastline.

We've Left Them

Embers are glowing
only brittle remains as
blankets for the little
and from lips, stomachs
blood is flowing
they're sideways falling
and mothers and fathers
are crawling to
their kids to find an
unrequited meeting
treasured moments
are fleeting
to God cry the feinting
and on the cheeks
of the hiccupping
doctors are painting blood
oh, here comes
the flood
of cinematic smoke
this world cares not
and we've left them to choke.

Is It Humane?

Is it humane
to be inhumane
towards another human
for being human?

The Children We Forgot

The eyes of a child
stop one in their tracks
but the news sells lies
forget the facts
the child lost their parents
the child lost their home
the child lost their freedom
they're shot if they roam
these children cry tears
the world can't comprehend
yet the ones who cause them
the world can't reprehend
so long as we say nothing
these children will keep dying
we cannot keep supporting
the side who keeps on lying.

Regrets

What could I say
how could I touch
when they had years before
been buried away?
Agony is such…

Tear Trails

If tears left trails
I would be honoured to learn
where you came from
and where you are yet
to venture
for my tears wish
to accompany you.

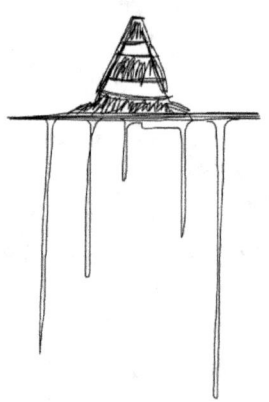

Blood

We all bleed the same colour,
but it shouldn't take
killing people to see that.
Sadly, we never learn anyway.

The Ways Of Our World

Can we not see
their unbelieving eyes
we knock the wings
of precious butterflies
and walk the earth
as the unnoticed
life form dies
their frosted lips
have words to say
but they're incapable
of movement
as their life decays
oh, the ways of
our world
and our thirst
for hurting
watch the world
and you'll see it working.

Family

I shot you
you shot me
we forgot
we're family.

Bare Minimum

I guess that's where we like to stay
safe and happy in shallow bay
while we keep hearts pending
for a love we're never sending
thinking it's okay.

Little Dreamer

And here we find
our little dreamer
circling under the sky
because she believes
that nothing can deter her believing
little dreamer,
the people who say
it can never be done
are those who forget
human potential
enough passion gets us places
and you certainly have enough
never let their remarks fracture you
little dreamer
for you believe in believing
but if you don't one day,
I will remind you that
there are places waiting
for souls like you
little dreamer
you will find the place you long for
so start with your heart
that's one place
that will always be there.

Falling

Falling out
of world
falling into
new
falling over me
to fall back
into you
different though
we seem
we're the same
in how we give
it's no wonder
you had truly
changed
the way
in which I live.

Quietness

They fall quiet
to the beauty of your quietness
but even more so
when you prove to them
how you can change the world
with a single act
how could they not miss
the stunning power
you possess?
You're a fusion of so many
beautiful things
a dance of ember and snow,
ribbons and alpenglow
though you seem not to know…
Still, off you go
to set yourself and others free.

Genuine

Beautiful lives in what and who is genuine –
to love for love and not reward solely.

Wanting to
give
kindness,
but afraid
of being
watched

Wrongs And Rights

Disinterest is indicative of a lack of empathy.
Fear is indicative of withheld compassion.
We forgive outwardly expressed wrongs
by acknowledging internally held rights.

The answer was here the whole time

The Intuitive Heart

Perhaps it is that a heart which of social standing yearns
is soon a heart which of deeper value learns –
of true importance, hearts often know
before any inkling of second thoughts show.

Trends

Self-centred friends
is where real connection ends
it becomes far too lonely
when people worship trends.

Popularity

What is popular isn't fulfilling.
Think of what the act is instilling.
Through our empathy, it is drilling.
It's sad to watch groups soul killing.
-A good heart is never truly unpopular.

What Isn't Love?

Co-dependency isn't love.
Relationships are not about
completing one another, for
that is only up to us.
We must compliment each
other's traits and work
together to better ourselves.
When we attain peace
with who we are,
our lives, independence and
relationships we enter will be
a force for good, not bad.
This is imperative.

Quiet Presence, Present Mind

You think so little of me
but you have no idea
what I'm capable of
throw me aside
and I'll resurrect
over and over and over
set fire in my way
and I'll walk right through it
you'll be lost for words
at how effortlessly
I make a comeback
but this isn't a show
it's just me letting you know
not to mess with a quiet soul
yes, I may be quiet
but a quiet presence
can have a present mind
so present that they know
exactly what's going on
and that should scare you
because I'm here to do
what's right.

"Look what
 I have"

Validation

Do we need validation?
We should have no
temptation for it
our values should be so strong
that we know where we belong
our independence is our power
there should never be an hour
where we crave to show off,
for that is no way to behave
a person isn't an exhibition
and using them as such
no doubt leads to suspicion
we should be fine operating alone,
and remember we're okay.
To have respect for others
should always be our way.

Do You Feel Incomplete?

When feeling incomplete, we tend to misread this emotion as a prompt for identifying with surface levels circumstances more. It's understandably tricky to catch the truth of this emotion, because our minds are so used to identifying with things like our job, income, popularity, academic achievements, etc. We think repeating those kinds of things to others and ourselves will fix this confusion in identity, but we are only fooling ourselves. It's what lies deep in our hearts that will truly give us the answer to who we are. The love we feel when immersed in the hobby or sport we love. When we are in solitude. When we reunite with nature. When we give charity, live charity. Feel the wind, share conversations that feel rare and inspiring. Like a call to action, because it is. And it's not something that should be hard. This isn't about forcing identity - we already fall back into who we are when we engage with the aforementioned things, or whichever things you personally love. It's just that a lot of the time we don't realise that these are keys to self-understanding. We miss the answer whilst we're engaging with the answer all the time. Don't be afraid of dropping the surface level identity you repeat to others. The real answers you seek are already with you. You need only look within.

~~Threat~~

Friend

Fear

If you fear yourself,
you will fear those
around you.
If you don't fear yourself,
you'll find no need to
fear or harm those
around you.

Who I should be is me

Finding

I know not yet
of who I am
despite knowing
who I am
who I should be
in this world
is me
and who I could
become is not entirely
unknown.

You are ENOUGH

Liberation

There was no greater joy
than knowing that I could
liberate myself
simply by embracing the soul
I never chose to shake hands with.

~~Topic Sentence
Evidence
Elaboration
Link to thesis~~

MY
THESIS:

The Education System

Creative expression
is the pathway to depression
because school places oppression
on an open mind's expression
-a prompt for educational reform.

The Day

Might it be beautiful, the day
when I stand by a door
that doesn't cast me out
for years on end
as it did before.

Powerful And Beautiful

The world we see
can look disheartening sometimes
and an appreciation for good deeds
has been lost by some people
but as the world keeps turning
so too does my head over my shoulder
for I know a love is still nestled within us
I shall listen in the silence,
and I shall feel when no one else will
there are many worlds to one
and to give my heart and all
is to inspire hope in this world
regardless of hate, anger, fear
because to love others
is something powerful, and beautiful.

Embrace what makes you stronger

Difficulties

Difficulties are just as essential
as they are beautiful –
at the time, a question,
and in the future,
a nod of the head.

Adversity is a gift

Forgiving The Situation

In our lives, it is so imperative that we learn to forgive. If we know someone has made a genuine mistake, we can forgive them. If someone constantly hurts us though, that's when we need to assess the pattern, assess the person's values and look into stepping away. But what if we're having tremendous trouble forgiving? What if our heart is in so much pain and our lungs are so heavy that we feel we could never forgive them? That they have done the worst thing possible? We may not forgive them here, but we must learn a new way of perceiving the situation. Circumstances such as these are inevitable in life, there's no evading them. They are powerfully hurtful but powerfully informative. Forgiving the situation is forgiving what life comes with. Forgiving the situation is accepting that everything is all part of a plan. The tests and trials we are faced with are necessary – they appear to see whether we hold a grudge and lash back or forgive the person and develop our soul - which can even help others do so.

Do we really want to live our lives being pessimistic towards the people who did wrong? Do we really want our grudges to take hold of how our day goes? Take a step back, assess. Forgive the person, forgive the situation, forgive yourself.

Hatred

For every hatred outward
is often a hatred inward
so instead of responding hatefully
always promote compassion
it can change social environments
and the hearts that walk through them.

People Want To Hear Negativity

The peace you feel when responding to someone respectfully or even not at all is lovely. Wishing them well can feel even better. It's not about claiming to be the better person because you 'did the better thing' either. It's actually about recognising one's humanity. They may not be showing theirs at this point in time, but that's probably because it's so buried that even they have trouble accessing it themselves. Forgiving what they haven't worked on is one of the most enlightening emotions one can experience. It's very insightful and helps us communicate - and live - in far better ways.

Remember: people want to hear negativity in a fight.

Don't feed either of your egos.

Our Precious Languages

We are so blessed to be able to speak a language. And it may not be something that crosses our minds that often. But if we have this gift to speak a language of such complexity, such depth, then we are responsible to use it in a respectful way. There are far too many good words to put to waste, and far too many reasons to be kind to one another. This precious gift of language is far greater and important than we care to realise. We take it for granted every day. Let's work towards being conscious of this gift and of speaking to others well. Too often do we see poor words being spoken, and it is especially frightening if they are spoken by higher authorities - for we learn it and pass it on.

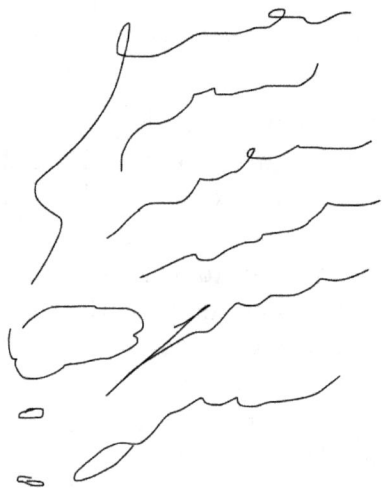

To Listen Properly

Erase response
from the mind
as one speaks;
it only undoes
what the other person
has taken the time to say.

Learning Your Language

Please
don't depend on my language
I don't want the unnecessary weight
put on you
to meet me exactly
on my end
let me meet you halfway
let me learn your language
some people probably never think to
because it's not in our curriculum
it's not deemed important
but is for me
and I will do it for you
I will spend this time for you.

Colours

It's a shame that
the gorgeous colour palette
you have is thought to be
unattractive - that's
a complete lie
you are stunningly bold,
absolutely beautiful
and leave so many in awe.

A Common Dismissal

It is sad to wonder of the common dismissal that what we think is not is perhaps what is.

Culture

The Western world likes to think
that their way is the only way
that their culture should be
an example for the rest of world
but it's clear the damage
they have caused
has it never occurred to
Western society
that beautiful practices
in cultures other than theirs
can also lead to happiness?

Misconception

If we see something everyday
it goes over our heads,
but if we don't see something everyday
it gets to our heads.

All It Took

All it took them was sharing a meal alongside the brothers
and sisters they never saw as brothers or sisters.
All it took them was walking into their place of worship and
realising just how welcoming the community was.
All it took was someone wishing peace upon them to realise
the peace they never thought to wish upon others.
In the end, their heart was so humbled by what they initially
thought was threatening that they stepped forth.
The light of truth overcame fear.
They embraced.
Their world changed.
And they helped change the world.

A Captive Life

Our minds are fogged because of lies
that consequently reform our eyes
and in this trouble lies
the demise of our own perception…
deception can steal our hold
of our identity, and we will
live our lives captive
often without even knowing.

Mixed Race

Too white to be brown
yet too brown to be white
such a crisis of identity
in this ongoing fight
but I refuse to be told
I belong to neither side
for I represent diversity,
and that I hold with pride
a planet lives within me
and my features tell the truth
of a child who was rejected
over looks that gave no proof
of being 'full enough' for them
we're supposed to be
a community
so how is it that we still don't
know how to embrace unity?
Such a crisis of identity
yet here I stand right now
you tell me I don't qualify
but I still say we're family.

Judgement

Sometimes it's not that we're
at war with ourselves,
but rather, we're at war
with the idea of judgement
from everyone but ourselves.

Let's Move Forth Together

The healing art of writing these
is how reflection invites ease
I'm healing me, and perhaps you
and potentially even someone new
our souls transform through
each lesson we learn
it stings a little, but in return
we find our minds a lot more clear
it's worth our pain, and worth our tear
I value your sadness as much as mine
so let's move forth together.

Heartbeat

Listen to my heart beat,
and I will remind you
that yours does too.

To Truly Live

Selflessness doesn't take
so much as it gives
and for someone to have
a heart like that
means they truly live.

Ballet Steps

Upside down sky
spinning round
and round
ballet steps
begin to run
and float above
the ground.

Soulmate Dance

Take my hand
and dance with me
we are too afraid
to look each other
in the eyes
but I have
a faint idea
of what emotion
lies in your heart
yet you seem to
tell lies
and that makes
me smile
for we drag out
the while
in knowing who
loves who
whilst falling
in love more
it's you I adore
I am enamoured by you.

Where I Fall Weak for You

Waltz with me
in slow motion
rest, my dear
sway as emotion
does when thou
fall gentle now
and cry your fears
without a sound
so rest your cheek
upon my heart
where I fall weak for you.

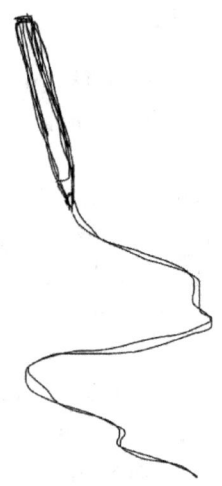

Written

To the person I am written for,
I am excited to meet you one day.
I am excited to feel
the understanding we will
have for one another.
For the look in your eyes
and the values in your heart
for your support, your guidance
and that I may fall into your arms.
I am excited to be yours
and for you to be mine
for us to be a passionate force for good,
and to better one another.
You will be my inspiration
just as I hope to be yours.
The longing in my heart to hear
your own only grows with time.
Until then, we must be patient,
but know that I miss you every day.
One day, God willing, we will
unite and recognise one another.
It is a beautiful thing to be written for each other.
Sincerely,
Your awaiting love.

Make Peace

Make peace with not knowing -
not everything is meant to be known,
and if we trust this reality, we will find peace.

Courage

Let there
arise within you
courage
in the pain of this moment
that accepts
life as it comes
and falls in love
with what's in store
a few tears
are okay
but let it not
see you collapse
into sleep
nor wither away
love waits gently
for you to take
a few steps more
so take them.

A message for you

The Truth About Trials

It's not happening TO us.
It's happening FOR us.
Our trials are given to us for a reason.
If we fail to understand this,
we fail to activate our potential for
a more optimistic way of life.

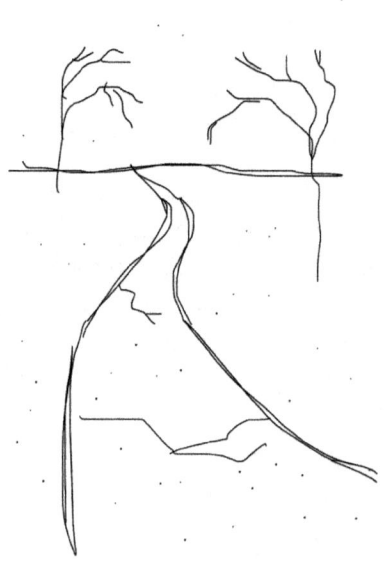

The Path We Are Afraid To Take

When a path is meant for you,
your heart is notified in a
highly spiritual way
it is felt on a level like
no other,
and it asks of no delay
but sometimes we feel
reluctant to walk it right away
as we may fear failure
or someone may be stopping
us from taking it
and as painful as these setbacks
may feel, it must never prevent
us from living the life
we are destined for.
Fulfil your heart's calling,
not the desires of others -
or else your life will be lived
walking further and further along
the completely wrong path.

The Heart And Mind

If the heart can rationalise,
then the mind can emote.

Time

The invention
of the clock
scared the stealth
of time
so much
that we now
fear time
instead of
appreciating it.

Blessing

Gratitude

The moment we realise the gratitude we have not been giving
our mind cannot help but reflect on our entire life
and how long we have lived without acknowledging
every blessing we are blessed with -
the house we always enter
the food we always eat
the schools we always attend
the bed we always sleep in
and the safety we always enjoy
these are things we enjoy with only a few periods
of gratitude in between.
If we are fortunate enough to be privileged with these things,
it is only fair to give sincere and plentiful thanks for them
as there are many struggling hearts across the world
who wish exactly for what we take for granted.

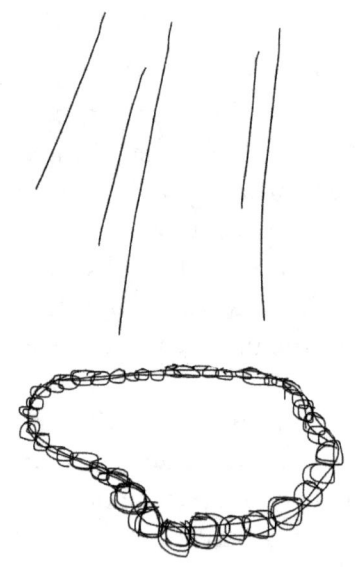

The Beauty Of Prayer

An entire world is being acknowledged
in a single string of emotional words
blessings are sent upon those we know and do
not know, and those we are yet to know
a moment to give thanks, an opportunity
to look inward at our behaviour, to
look outward in selflessness
to let out pain we are too afraid to
tell others, pain that others may not
quite understand
we find solace, we find answers,
we find ourselves, and our way back
to the path our heart needs.

The Trauma Identity

We tend to - even like to - think we are alone with what we're going through. If we trick ourselves into thinking we're the only one going through a particular adversity, we build a wall around us that blocks out any outside opinions. Because why would we want to let go of the precious story we have created for ourselves? If we chose to let go if it, then it would mean that we are 'letting go of who we are'. The mistake we are making is confusing adversity with identity. We are not our trauma. And moving on from trauma doesn't mean we've lost our identity. If anything, who we are blossoms. Trauma should help us grow, not keep us fixed in a moment in time. If we have lost someone, for instance, it isn't to say we let go of remembrance. However, loss isn't identity. If we identify with loss, the love and healing we seek will forever be out of reach. So what will it be?
Unending pain, or unending love?

Remember With Happiness

Confusing is the mixture of comforting and discomforting memories...
we see smiles turn to frowns instead of frowns turning to smiles. We see eyes
closing forever instead of eyes finding ours and reassuring us forever.
How weary the mind must be to constantly process such conflicting images.
We must, however, choose happiness. There is too much love to put to waste.
Smile the smile that they would smile to see on your face.

Sign Language

I may never see
my friend again
but that shall be okay.
His presence is off
somewhere far,
but his signs will forever stay.

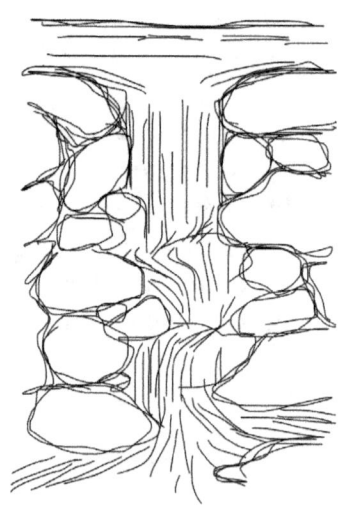

Inspiration And Solace

I find it beautiful
that the both of us
simultaneously knew
and did not know
of the astonishing ways
in which we
inspired and found solace
in one another.

Just Like The Sun

And it snowed in my soul...
the cold lingered,
but my tears soon dried -
for the prevailing warmth
of my heart restored me
just as the sun restores
the ground.

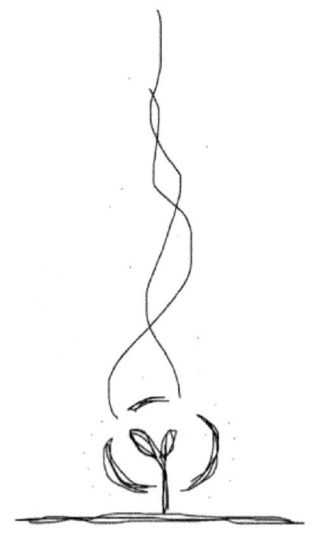

Time To Grow

For all these things
that hurt us so
are the lessons
we adopt when
it's time to grow
time to go.

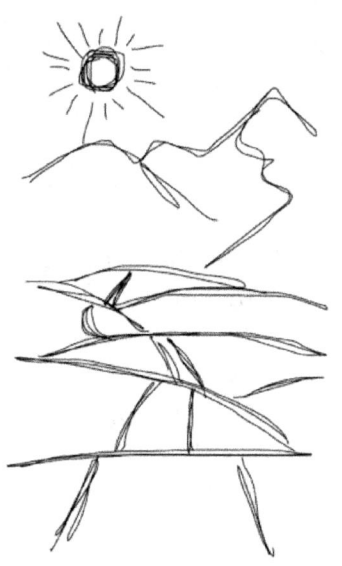

A Bird In Flight

You may have wondered where I am
well, I'm off somewhere far now
running towards the mountains
I was too afraid to climb
towards the road I was
too afraid to take
and to the dawn I was too afraid
to believe in
my tears are flying in the wind
my arms outstretched as though a bird in flight
and I will one day tell you
all about my wonderful adventure
to this momentous day.

Possible

And were it not possible,
I wouldn't
have dreamt
the impossible
and done
the impossible
so as to call
it possible.

Now

We've reflected on so much, but eventually comes the time to act. Don't be afraid of what your heart is trying to communicate to you. Often times the heart is told to wait with the truth it's holding because we didn't understand the truth at first, or we didn't want to listen to it. But the heart knows what is best, and so it will continue to send you prompts for reflection to remind you to look inward. To not be afraid of looking inward. How can we be afraid of what is truly good for us? Being brave by reflecting is far better than ignoring what we need. The heart frowns when we ignore it because it's trying to give us the very key to the happiness we're trying to find. We only have now, yet we assume we have the future. The future isn't promised, but our heart holds the key to getting there. By learning to love your heart, you will understand and accept the truths it gives to you more and more. Eventually, you will have no trouble endeavouring on the path meant for you. Be excited for your happiness. Be excited for this wonderful journey.

Acknowledgements

I would like to extend my thanks to my parents,
who have raised me beautifully and supported the person
I have become today.
To my friends, you are all a huge part of my life and I'm so grateful
for the smiles, lessons and compassion you bring.
And to those who are reading this book,
your time and support mean so much.
I hope this book has provided healing and inspiration for you.

About The Author

Ella Zelensky is a poet, current university student in anthropology and is of a mixed-race background. Since she was young, culture, race, religion, language, cinematography and activism have played a major role in her creative work and academic studies. After struggling with fitting in during her early high school years, writing poetry helped her get through and rise above. Eventually, writing became serious to her and she began sharing her work on her social media platform. Her dream to be a humanitarian worker, as well as interests in education, mental health and equality inspire many of her poems and quotes. Through Ella's passion for people, reform and harmony, she wishes to help others own their identity, take a stand, forgive, unite, and ultimately heal.

www.ellazelensky.com

www.ingramcontent.com/pod-product-compliance
Lightning Source LLC
Chambersburg PA
CBHW051357290426
44108CB00015B/2046